Canadian
Wild Flowers
and Emblems

By Colleayn O. Mastin  *Illustrated by Jan Sovak*

*G*rasshopper
BOOKS PUBLISHING

A portion of the sales of this book will be donated to the Canadian Nature Federation

Indian Pipe

A spooky plant called Indian pipe
In the gloomy forest is found;
It looks as if some smokers
Shoved their pipes into the ground.

This plant, when young, is pale and white,
Dark brown when it is ripe.
An eerie, ancient, strange plant
Is the ghostly Indian pipe!

This ghostly flower pokes its head through the forest floor in early summer. It will turn black, and ooze a jelly like substance if it is touched.

This plant is a parasite, so it must get its food from dead or decaying plants. The Indian pipe cannot make its own food because it does not have the green coloring, called chlorophyll that is usual in other plants.

Indian pipe grows in the deep moist forests all across Canada. It is a very old plant and has been used in folk medicine to treat sore eyes and nervous troubles. Its other names are ghost plant, fairy smoke, and corpse plant.

Lady Slipper

Provincial Flower of Prince Edward Island

Isn't it odd that a flower
That looks like the slipper of a lady,
Should choose to live in bogs and swamps,
And places both muddy and shady?

And there's something else surprising:
Though each lady slipper is small,
The plants on which we find them
Are really rather tall.

Many people believe that the orchid is
among the most exquisite of the world's
flowers. The lady slipper is a member of
this family, and like all orchids, needs
special conditions to grow.

The seeds are very small and though
they are produced in great numbers,
it may take as long as fifteen years
for a seed to grow into a flowering plant.

This delicate plant is found from
Alberta to Prince Edward Island.
It was adopted as the floral emblem
of P.E.I in 1965.

Bird - Blue Jay
Tree - Red Oak

Arctic White Heather

A Nunavut flower

Up in the Arctic tundra,
Where winters are cold and dark,
This heather plant keeps out of the wind,
By creeping behind a rock.

The heather's white flowers are bell-shaped
And have a very sweet smell;
In spite of where it has chosen to live
Arctic heather survives very well.

Both the Arctic White Heather and the saxifrage grow on the tundra. This is the huge area of treeless land in Canada's north between the polar sea and the treeline. Most of the plants there grow close to the ground.

The Arctic Heather grows in a vast creeping pattern across the land. It is among the most prolific plants on the tundra.

The stems contain resin, a sticky substance that oozes out and makes this plant easy to ignite. A small fire made with Arctic heather burns with a very hot flame. Within minutes, this hot fire can quickly boil a kettle of water. This is very important as there is no other readily available firewood.

The Inuktitut name is Qijuktaat, meaning wood that is ready to be gathered.

Purple Saxifrage

Saxifrage flowers are very small,
They're about the size of a pea,
But they can turn the tundra purple,
For as far as the eye can see.

There's something very unusual
About these purple plants:
Their stalks are hairy and sticky
To protect their pollen from ants.

The blooming of this plants indicates to the people of the north that the young caribou will soon be born. It is one of the first plants to flower when the snow recedes.

The name "saxifrage" means "stone breaker". This is because people once thought this tiny flower was strong enough to make the cracks in the rocks where they often grow.

In communities where there are not many edible berries, people eat the purple flowers. The flower is also called Aupillatinguat, meaning like blood spots. The plant has been used to make tea and medicine.

Bleeding Heart

Bleeding hearts sprout in shady woods,
Sometime between March and May;
There lovely flowers are pale and red
And their leaves are green or gray.

The bleeding heart has long brought joy
To the life of many a child;
The tame ones grow in our gardens,
While others grow tall and wild.

The bleeding heart was given its name because on the tip of each of its drooping, heart-shaped flowers, there is a bright red spot.

Another member of the bleeding heart family also has a very odd name. It's called "Dutchman's breeches," because its flowers look like a baggy pair of pants. Unlike many wild flowers, bleeding hearts are not used for food or medicine.

Dogwood
Provincial Flower of B.C.

The dogwood's pale white flowers
Add beauty to this tree;
It's against the law to cut one
In the province of B.C.

The dogwood's blooms of summer
Are changed in early fall,
And become, as if by magic,
A bright red tiny ball.

The name "Dogwood" has nothing to do with dogs, but comes from "Dagge", an early English word meaning "sharp and pointed." Since the wood of this tree is very hard, people used to make sharp things like skewers and wedges out of it.

It is only near the ocean on Vancouver Island, and on the mainland of B.C. that your will find this flowering tree. The fruit is very important to wildlife, especially birds. Deer also feed on the twigs and leaves of this tree.

It was adopted in 1956 as British Columbia's flower.

Bird - Stellar's Jay
Tree - Western red cedar

Kinnikinnick

Bearberry is another name
For the kinnikinnick shrub,
And many hungry bears agree
Its fruit makes tasty grub.

In spring, the kinnikinnick
Has blossoms shaped like a bell;
In autumn, these flowers turn into
The berries bears like so well.

Foxes, coyotes, birds, and bears eat the bright red berries, while deer are very fond of the leathery leaves that grow on this low-lying shrub. Even in the winter, the leaves can be dug from under the snow and eaten.

Because kinnikinnick berries are dry and powdery, most people don't like them, but they can be chewed to prevent thirst. The leaves can also be used to make a pale green, mild-tasting tea. This beautiful evergreen plant is found growing in great hectare beds from Labrador to the Yukon.

The cranberries we eat at Thanksgiving and Christmas look very similar to the kinnikinnick berry. People often mistake one berry for the other.

Mountain Avens

Floral Emblem of the Northwest Territories

This mountain plant is an evergreen
With leaves as tough as leather;
Its home is in the Arctic,
It likes sunny, cold, cold weather.

At summer's end, its flowers
Turn into a feathery ball,
And is carried along on the north wind
Until its seeds all fall.

Mountain Avens are heliotropic. This means that during the day, their flowers follow the path of the sun across the sky. Because these flowers face the sun, they act like solar collectors and are a favorite place for insects to perch in order to get warm.

This is a very special flower in the Canadian Arctic. It sometimes grows in vast colorful carpets across the tundra. Everyone knows these plants, and with their creamy yellow flowers are a welcome sight after the long, cold winter.

The Inuit call the mountain aven, Malikaat, which means "the follower," because it follows the sun around the sky.

This flower grows from Newfoundland to the Yukon, from the high alpine to the Arctic Circle.

Bird - Gyr Falcon
Tree - Jack Pine

Fireweed

Floral Emblem of the Yukon

After loggers have cleared the land,
Or a forest fire roared by,
The fireweed plant springs quickly up.
With stems two metres high.

The ripened seeds of fireweed,
Float like parachutes through the air,
These seeds of fireweed travel far,
Look around, they're everywhere.

In the fall, the soft downy seeds of the
fireweed are carried through the air to
produce these beautiful flowers in the
Yukon, Northwest Territories, Nunavut,
and other areas across most of Canada.
New plants are also produced when
shoots from the roots push up through
the earth.

These young shoots and flower buds
can be eaten raw or boiled, and used
as a medicine. The flowers are a favorite
collecting spot for bees, and the resulting
honey is highly prized for its sweet smell
and excellent taste.

Fireweed plants are among the first one
to sprout and grow in burned over areas.
It became the floral emblem of the Yukon
in 1957.

Bird - Common Raven

Harebell

The harebell hangs its bell-shaped blooms
On stems both thin and long;
This plant may look quite delicate,
But it's really very strong.

It grows above the timberline,
Or close to a mountain stream;
It's also found on the barren shores
Where the winds of the Arctic scream.

The harebell is another name for the "Bluebell of Scotland." This beautiful blue flower is famous all over the world in story and particularly in the song, "The Bluebells of Scotland."

This strong, rugged plant can withstand many temperature changes. It grows from Labrador to British Columbia.

Oxeye Daisy

In June, when school is over,
Out pops the oxeye daisy:
It tells us summer has arrived
When days are long and lazy.

These daisies' shining faces
Point always at the sun;
This flower we call "The eye of day"
Is known by everyone.

For years and years, the white petals of
the daisy have been plucked off one at a
time to help people decide whether "he
(or she) loves me or loves me not."

The name oxeye comes from the white
and yellow flowers that look like the
great fringed eye of an oxen. The young
leaves of this plant can be used in salads.

Wild Rose

Provincial Flower of Alberta

The soft and dark-pink petals
Of the prickly wild rose
Add beauty to the pastures
And the roadsides where it grows.

The rosehips found each autumn
Are good for jam or tea;
They taste just great, and are full of
The vitamin we call "C".

From all the beautiful wild flowers that grow across Alberta, the school children chose the wild rose as its provincial flower in 1930. These flowers are found growing from Saskatchewan to British Columbia.

The petals of the wild rose produce an oil that can be used to make perfume. These petals can also be sugared and made into candy.

After the petals have fallen from the flower, the part that remains is called a rosehip. These berries are an important winter food for many birds. Bears also eat the rosehips before they take their long winter sleep.

Early settlers and native people used the rosehip for food and to make tasty jelly and jams. Many early explorers owed their lives to the berries and nuts they were able to find from the many wild plants that grow across Canada.

Bird - Great Horned Owl
Tree - Lodgepole Pine

Mayflower

Floral Emblem of Nova Scotia

The mayflower is dainty and fussy,
It won't grow just anywhere,
But when it blooms and blossoms,
A sweet smell fills the air.

This creeping flower likes to be
Near trees that are evergreen;
It blossoms in late winter,
When snow can still be seen.

The mayflower is also called trailing arbutus or ground laurel. This pretty flower grows from Labrador to Saskatchewan.

It was named by the pilgrims, who saw it as the first flower of spring, and as a sign that their first terrible winter was over. The "Mayflower" was the name of the ship that brought the pilgrims to North America.

It became Nova Scotia's official flower in 1907.

Bird - Osprey
Tree - Red Spruce

Buttercup

Some buttercups grow sort of short,
While others grow quite tall,
Though sunny yellow flowers
Are found upon them all.

Fields of golden buttercups
Are thought to look just great,
But if they creep into our gardens,
They are weeds we learn to hate.

If a friend tickles you under the chin with a buttercup and your chin turns yellow, it means, according to folklore, that you like butter.

Out in the pastures, cows usually don't eat buttercups because they have a bitter taste. But if they do, the milk they produce does not taste good. Buttercups grow all across Canada.

Red Lily

Saskatchewan's Provincial Flower

The red or prairie lily
Is sometimes seen to tower
Above the prairie grasses,
With its single, cup-shaped flower.

It also likes the open woods.
You might see some lilies there,
But because of over-picking,
They are now becoming rare.

These beautiful lilies were once a common sight, growing in great numbers across meadows, fields, and forests from Quebec to B.C. But because of over-picking, and being destroyed by grazing cattle, they are now difficult to find.

This plant grows from a bulb which first nations peoples and early Canadian settlers thought made a good substitute for potatoes.

Red lilies are now a protected species, and no one is allowed to pick them. It was named Saskatchewan's provincial flower in 1941.

Bird - Sharptailed Grouse
Tree - White Birch

Queen Anne's Lace

The flower known as Queen Anne's Lace
Is known by another name:
It's called a "wild carrot,"
Though the carrots we eat are tame.

Among its pale white blossoms,
There one that's pink or brown;
This blossom makes a target,
For insects flying down.

It is not known which of several Queens called Anne gave her name to this flower. One story says that the red spot in the middle of the flower, represents a drop of blood that fell from the Queen's hand while she was making lace.

The carrot-like roots of this plant are edible, but be careful: they look similar to a poisonous plant called water hemlock. Queen Anne's Lace is a very common plant found all over the world.

Pitcher Plant

Provincial Flower of Newfoundland

The pitcher plant that grows in bogs
Is a rare carnivorous plant;
This means it likes to have for lunch
A spider, a fly, or an ant.

The way it gets such meaty food
Is very smart, no doubt:
Insects slide down its hollow leaves,
Then find they can't fly out.

This is no ordinary plant; it eats insects. Its hollow leaves have downward-pointing bristles that make it easy for insects to slide down into the leaf, but very hard for them to escape and make their way back up to freedom.

The flower looks like an umbrella and the stems look like a pitcher or a jug with a handle. They grow in bogs and marshes in Newfoundland, Labrador, and the Northwest Territories.

Queen Victoria chose the pitcher plant as a design for a penny. It was later chosen as the floral emblem of Newfoundland.

Bird - Puffin
Tree - Black Spruce

Dandelion

When the yellow head of a dandelion
Turns into a fuzzy ball,
The dandelion is ready for
A wind or a breeze to call.

Because of the way it spreads its seeds,
It is found all over the globe;
In the early spring, the fields are dressed
In a beautiful, golden robe.

Many people like to add the young leaves or roots of the dandelions to a salad. Or how about a dandelion sandwich made from tender dandelion leaves, bread and butter with a sprinkle of salt?

For centuries, children have played many games with dandelions. By counting how many times you have to blow to clear all the heads off a "fuzzy," you can tell what time it is. This also helps to spread the seeds of nature's most common wildflower.

The name "dandelion" means "tooth of a lion". It probably gets this name because the jagged edges of a dandelion leaf look like lions' teeth.

Trillium

Provincial Flower of Ontario

The white trillium has three petals,
That sit on a three-leafed ring;
This flower is a woodland plant
That brightens up the spring.

As March days slip away to May,
These white flowers turn to pink;
Sometimes they turn magenta,
Which is purplish-red, I think.

It takes about six years for this lovely plant to produce its first bloom. If the leaves of the white trillium are picked along with the flower, then the plants die. This beautiful flower is protected, and it is illegal to pick it.

"Tri" means three and this is how this plant with three petals and three leaves got its name. It does have another name, the "Wake Robin" because it comes out so early in the spring.

It grows all across Ontario and became it's floral emblem in 1937.

Bird - Common Loon
Tree - White Pine

Jewelweed

The jewelweed has a special way
Of scattering all its seeds:
Its ripened pods pop open,
Then scatter their tiny "beads."

The jewelweed is a summer plant,
It blossoms in mid-July,
But it cannot stand cold weather:
At first-frost they wither and die.

The hummingbird with its long bill is the only bird that can reach the pollen deep in the jewelweed's flower. Bees cannot reach the pollen, even though they can collect the nectar, but this does not help to pollinate the flower.

To scatter its bead-like seeds, the jewelweed suddenly pops open and its seeds fly in every direction. In this way many new plants will be spread over a wide area. It is thought that this flower was given its name because the bright orange flowers that dangle from it, look like colorful earrings or jewels.

If you touched some poison ivy, you could rub the itchy spot with jewelweed leaves to take away the itch. Some tribes used this plant to treat skin itches and athlete's foot.

Sunflower

In a farmer's field or garden,
Tame sunflowers grow quite tall,
Though the wild ones are much shorter,
About two metres high, that's all.

A wild sunflower grows many heads,
While the garden type has one;
Both flowers like to spend each day,
Staring blindly at the sun.

Garden sunflowers have gigantic heads, while wild sunflowers have smaller heads and grow along roadsides and in fields. They are found all across Canada.

To protect themselves, sunflower plants release a poison which stops other plants from growing near them. Native indians used the seeds to make sunflower oil and flour. The seeds are delicious to eat.

The pith of the sunflower is the lightest natural substance known. It is even lighter than cork. Some farmers think that feeding sunflower seeds to chickens will help them to lay more eggs.

Garden Lily

Floral Emblem of Quebec

This lily is not a wild plant,
But has been included here,
Because in Quebec, La Belle Provence,
This flower is held so dear.

This tender-looking lily,
With blooms of waxy-white,
Can sometimes even grow outside,
And reaches one metre in height.

Because this ancient lily
has long been associated
with Mary, the Mother of Jesus,
it is also called the Madonna
or Lent Lily.

Though its flowers appear in June or July,
this lily's long green leaves do not show
up until autumn. This lovely, pure white
lily is easy to grow. Its blossoms are beautiful.

It was chosen as the floral emblem of
Quebec in 1963.

Bird - Snowy Owl
Tree - Yellow Birch

Violet

Provincial Flower of New Brunswick

In dark, damp woods or meadows,
Violets don't grow very high;
Their five leaves grouped together
Are shaped like a butterfly.

This flower has been a favorite
For many and many a year;
On all the earth's vast continents,
These purple flowers appear.

If you can imagine eating a flower, look no further! These beautiful springtime flowers, can be eaten raw in salads, fried in butter, added to soup, or coated with sugar to make a kind of candy. Like the petals of the wild rose, they are rich in Vitamin C.

Some people used to believe that a handkerchief soaked in violet water and placed on the forehead would take away a headache.

These violets grow from New Brunswick to Manitoba. It became New Brunswick's floral emblem in 1936.

Bird - Black Capped Chickadee
Tree - Balsam Fir

Marsh Marigold

When marsh marigolds flower in spring,
It means that winter's over;
The farmer knows he can now begin
To start planting some crops like clover.

The marigold's flowers are yellow,
But its leaves are the color of cream;
It feels at home in a soggy spot,
And can even take root in a stream.

Marsh marigolds are not afraid to grow in the middle of a stream or in a shallow river. They are among the few wildflowers that can survive in marshes or along roadside ditches.

These deep yellow-orange flowers are the first bright blossoms to appear in the spring. They bloom from April to June all across Canada. In earlier times, it was the custom for people to spread the flowers around the front door of their houses.

Some people use the boiled leaves of the marsh marigold as a vegetable. But the leaves must be boiled first. They can be poisonous if eaten raw. Other people thought this plant provided a cure for warts.

The petals produce a yellow dye which can be used to color clothes and fabrics. Other names for this plant are king-cup and cowslip.

Crocus

Provincial Flower of Manitoba

The prairie crocus must be brave
To push up through the snow,
To tell the cold and waiting world
That winter soon will go.

In spring, the prairie crocus
Has so many blooms in view,
That it makes the fields and meadows,
Look a lovely, smoky blue.

This brave flower pushes up through the earth in the early spring and blooms even before the snow has melted. These flowers are so numerous, they are sometimes called by another name, "prairie smoke."

The crocus can survive the cold spring weather with its rapid changes in temperature. Tiny hairs grow all over this plant, and act like a warm protective blanket. This keeps it from freezing while it waits for the warm spring sun.

Early settlers on the prairies used these purple flowers to make a dye to color Easter eggs. The children of Manitoba chose the prairie crocus as the province's official flower in 1906.

Bird - Great Grey Owl
Tree - White Spruce

Jack-in-the-Pulpit

You don't have to look very hard
To see how Jack got his name;
For a minister in his pulpit
Looks very much the same.

But natives saw Jack differently,
To them he was the rack,
On which an Iroquois mother
Held her baby on her back.

Be careful! The underground stem of this plant is very poisonous when eaten raw. But it is not poisonous when it is cooked, roasted, or dried. This plant, which was a common food among aboriginal people, has another name–Indian turnip.

The berries are eaten by woodland birds, but they are somewhat poisonous to humans. Jack-In-The-Pulpit is most commonly found growing from New Brunswick to Manitoba.

Bladderwort

When it comes to being exceptional,
The bladderwort earns a prize:
It grows on top of a lake or pond,
And eats bugs of any size.

As well as keeping it afloat,
The "bladders" of this plant
Are used to trap the insects
That fight to get free, but can't.

You can't blame the bladderwort for its eating habits. Plants have to have nitrogen to make them grow. Since bladderwort plants cannot get nitrogen from the water in which they live, they have to get it from the insects they capture.

When insects or larvae come too close, the tiny door of the trap opens, and the water carries the victim inside the plant. The door quickly closes and the insects or other organisms are digested by the bladderwort.

These plants live in slow moving ponds or lakes all across Canada.

Yellow Pond Lily

The yellow pond lily's flowers sit
Like crowns of shining gold,
On mats of heart-shaped lily-pads,
In water that's not too cold.

These heart-shaped leaves are handy rafts
For frogs that sunbathe there;
The thick green stems beneath the plants
Are food for the beaver and bear.

Creatures other than frogs that also like to use lily pads as a resting place are dragon flies and ducklings.

The underwater leaves of this lily are a good source of food for beavers and muskrats who can eat them all through the year.

Wild Strawberries

Some wildflowers are useful,
And some are good to eat;
Find some wild strawberries
If you'd really like a treat.

From flowers we can make perfumes,
Spices, oils and wine,
Or poisons, dyes and medicine,
And teas that taste just fine.

There are books written about the many wild plants and flowers that are both tasty and nourishing. Before you start eating wild plants, you should get advice from someone who knows which are safe and which might be poisonous.

These wild strawberries are eaten by robins, turtles, bears, mice and many other wild animals. The First Nations peoples used the berries to make jam and also used the leaves to make tea.

Strawberries grow low on the ground and spread along the ground on runners.

About twenty-five percent of all our medicines are made from plants.

Canadian Wildflowers & Emblems
Text copyright © 1997 by Colleayn O. Mastin
Illustration copyright © 1997 Jan Sovak

Published by Grasshopper Books Publishing
106 - Waddington Drive
Kamloops, B.C. V2E 1M2

This book is dedicated to Helen Evans and Helen and Jim Holden

Acknowledgements
The author wishes to thank the following:
Government of Canada, Guy Frenette, Jardin Botanique du Montreal, Judy Farrow, Karen McLaren, Wendy Nankievell, Wendy Hindle Dennis Johnson who is always so supportive.

Designed by Kunz+Associates
Printed in Canada by Friesen Printers Ltd. Altona, Manitoba

Canadian Cataloguing in Publication Data

Mastin, Colleayn O. (Colleayn Olive)
Canadian wildflowers and emblems

(Nature Canada Series; 8)
Includes index
ISBN 1-895910-16-1 (bound)--ISBN 1-895910-18-8 (pbk.)

1. Wildflowers--Canada--Juvenile literature, I. Sovak, Jan, 1953- II. Title. III. Series: Mastin, Colleayn O. (Colleayn Olive), - Nature Canada series ; 8.
QK201.M379 1997   j582.13'0971   C96-910709-9

INDEX:

Provincial Flowers